POETICA 38

Boethius: *Fortune's Prisoner*

By James Harpur

JAMES HARPUR

Fortune's Prisoner

THE POEMS OF BOETHIUS'S
Consolation of Philosophy

Anvil Press Poetry

Published in 2007
by Anvil Press Poetry Ltd
Neptune House 70 Royal Hill London SE10 8RF
www.anvilpresspoetry.com

This book is published with financial assistance
from Arts Council England

Designed and set in Monotype Bembo by Anvil
Printed and bound in England
by Cromwell Press, Trowbridge, Wiltshire

ISBN 978 0 85646 403 4

A catalogue record for this book
is available from the British Library

Contents

Acknowledgements

POEMS IN THIS collection have previously been published or accepted for publication in the following periodicals: *Cork Literary Review, Oxford Magazine, PN Review, Poetry Ireland Review, Southword.*

Many thanks to: Peter and Kit, Pat, Evie and Grace, Derek Robinson, and David Caulfield for his comments and encouragement; my old Latin teachers, Tim Hole of Wallop School, Weybridge, and Christopher Richardson and Stephen Winkley of Cranleigh School, for getting me started many years ago; and the director, administrator and staff of Hawthornden Castle for a fellowship during which most of this book was drafted.

Foreword

I FIRST BECAME interested in Boethius while studying English at university – specifically Chaucer's *Troilus and Criseyde*, a work imbued with Boethius's ideas and which Chaucer began writing at about the same time he was finishing his own translation of *The Consolation of Philosophy*. Notions of fate, fortune, free will, chance, coincidence, etc. had always fascinated me, and Boethius wrote about them in a compelling way. Many years later I decided to translate the poems from the *Consolation*'s prosimetric text (i.e. alternating prose and verse), and the result is this book. I was aware that extracting the poems might be like 'plucking pulses from a body'. But there are advantages too: taken from the amplified context of the prose (which I have summarized in an appendix), the poems gain from the protracted intensity of poetic imagination carried over, uninterrupted, poem by poem.

My translation is intended for readers of poetry as much as for classicists, philosophers, and other Boethius enthusiasts. So I have taken the liberty of giving the poems titles that did not exist in the original Latin (the poems are usually just labelled 'Book 1, metrum 1' etc. – 'metrum' meaning verse section or poem). I have done this for a number of reasons: to suggest the poem's theme and provide a little orientation; for ease of reference in the introduction; and to make the book feel more like a poetry collection. Beneath each poem there is a reference to the Latin text, for example 2 m.4 (i.e. Book 2, metrum 4).

9

In addition, I have appended epigraphs to many of the poems. A few of these are taken from the prose sections of the *Consolation*, when I thought some context might be helpful. Others are from a variety of sources and are intended to emphasize the theme or to complement it, as well as to show that Boethius was part of a philosophical and spiritual tradition extending backwards and forwards from his time: indeed it was one of his greatest achievements that he preserved and transmitted this tradition. Needless to say, the epigraphs do not necessarily indicate a direct influence either on, or issuing from, Boethius. In translating the poems I have not tried to mimic Boethius's wide range of verse forms. My method was to start with a rough translation then let the English form suggest itself organically.

Above all, it is my hope that this book might prompt readers to seek out or return to the *Consolation*, or to modern studies of it, some of which are listed in the select bibliography. My gratitude goes to all the translators and commentators who have made Boethius explicable and such a fascinating subject, particularly H. Chadwick, Gerard O'Daly, J. J. O'Donnell, Joel C. Relihan, P. G. Walsh and V. E. Watts. The Latin text I used was that edited by J. J. O'Donnell, along with the Loeb text of S. J. Tester.

Introduction

IN ABOUT AD 524, Anicius Manlius Severinus Boethius, a middle-aged Roman aristocrat, scholar, philosopher and Christian theologian and one of the most influential members of the court of Theodoric, the Ostrogothic ruler of Italy, was arrested for alleged treasonable activities against the king (see Appendix I). During his confinement at Pavia in northern Italy, Boethius, who faced the possibility of the death penalty, wrote his masterpiece, *The Consolation of Philosophy*, a work in which he considers universal issues such as the nature of justice, the problem of evil in a world controlled by God's providential plan, and the workings of Fortune and free will.

The book takes the form of a dialogue between Philosophy, who is personified as a woman, and the hapless Boethius, a prisoner bemoaning his fate. Philosophy sees it as her task to wean Boethius (or more correctly 'the prisoner' – Boethius's persona in the work) away from his destructive self-pity and to apply the soothing balm of reason to remedy his distress, which she views as a type of sickness. The book, which Edward Gibbon described as a 'golden volume not unworthy of the leisure of Plato or Tully [Cicero]', became one of the most influential works of the Middle Ages and beyond. It was translated by King Alfred the Great, Chaucer and Elizabeth I, among others. There were also versions made of it in Greek, medieval German, Middle Dutch, Italian and other languages. Dante, who was an avid reader of Boethius, refers to him in the *Paradiso* (X, 125) as 'the holy soul who brings to light the world's deceitfulness'.

Each of the *Consolation*'s five books (summarized in Appendix II) consists of prose alternating with poems (a form known as Menippean after the *Satires* of the third-century BC Greek writer Menippus of Gadara). In all there are thirty-nine poems: thirty-five of them are addressed by Philosophy to Boethius, while the remaining four are spoken by the prisoner himself. The poems serve to introduce, reflect, enlarge upon or emphasize the themes that the prose sections treat discursively.

Although the poems are naturally part of a unified whole, they also form a coherent thematic sequence by themselves. Under the magnifying lens of the poetic form, the *Consolation*'s themes retain a sharp focus. Problems of interpretation that occasionally arise in the poems are less to do with their being separated from the prose than the density and intricacy of ideas that Boethius, drawing on different classical traditions of thought, tries to convey within the limits of his chosen metres.

Although the poems can be enjoyed as individual units, it is as an extended sequence that they work best, since the echoes of their themes move back and forth from start to finish, illuminating and reinforcing the images and insights that arise. The journey starts with Boethius's abject, almost theatrical, distress and ends with Philosophy's words about the dignity of human beings and how their very body shape suggests they should be looking up towards the heavenly realm above, not down at the earth like the lower animals. Along the way there are poems about God and love, the falseness of earthly riches, the transience of human honours, the ascent of the soul to the realm of light, the slipperiness of Fortune, the laws of chance, and the nature of the mind and its modes of perception. By the end, the reader, like Bunyan's Pilgrim, has trekked through Boethius's slough of despond and come out the other side, his spirits lifted by the sense of transcendence that Philosophy has instilled. Boethius's consolation is Everyman's.

ESTIMATES OF Boethius's standing as a poet have varied over the centuries. Some have thought him sublime, others more of an adept versifier. The truth probably lies between the two. It is a question of whether the poems are felt to be merely vehicles that carry and parade his ideas and thoughts; or whether the latter have fused with his poetic imagination to create a unified whole in which ideas, language and form take life from each other.

At his best, Boethius is a subtle, artful and allusive poet, who draws on history and myth as well as a rich variety of symbols, metaphors and extended similes to illuminate his meaning. One of his strengths is his ability to express complex thoughts in memorable images. In, for example, Book 5 metrum 1, 'Law of Chance' (to reiterate: the original poems did not have titles) he sets out to illustrate the way that apparent occurrences of chance are in fact subsumed under a greater law of harmony. So he imagines the rivers Tigris and Euphrates uniting, with their flotsam and jetsam co-mingling and bumping along together, then points out that the seemingly haphazard collisions are in fact controlled by the shape of the terrain and the natural flow of the water: by analogy chance, which seems to operate on some random principle, does in fact obey the law.

Boethius is also extremely versatile. He can tell stories, crisply and succinctly, such as Orpheus's descent to Hades to rescue his dead wife Eurydice, or the bewitching of Ulysses's crew by the sorceress Circe; he can soliloquize with dramatic urgency; and he can write with delicate haiku-like brevity and suggestiveness, yoking disparate images to create his effect. Within a unifying voice he displays a wide range of tones, from coolness and sardonic wit to reverence and urgency. Also, behind the poems, even at their simplest, there is always a formidable intellect constantly exerting its pressure – probing, challenging, and seeking answers to the great mysteries of existence or attempting to elucidate them.

Although he had the mind of a philosopher, Boethius also had the heart of a Romantic and the soul of a Platonist, and some of his most moving lines are those that evoke a serene Platonic transcendence through images of the ordered universe, the cosmic rhythms of the sun, moon and stars, the glittering heavens, the harmony of the elements, and the pattern of the seasons. Equally, his detached observations and evocations can give way to moments of genuine heartfelt passion – not the histrionic self-pity of the opening poem – but in, say, 'Hymn to Creator' (3 m.9), a magnificent set-piece which lauds the father of the universe and his creation and ends with an imprecation to God for a vision of divine light; or in 'The Whole and Parts' (5 m.3), an insistent inner interrogation about the search for truth and the way the mind builds up a mental picture of reality.

IT IS DIFFICULT to distance the poems – as indeed the whole work – from Boethius's actual imprisonment. Anna Crabbe has referred to 'The real possibility of cold iron about the throat' giving 'a new dimension to a Christian Platonist's understanding of metaphysical shackles.'[1] And Gerard O'Daly has written: 'The *Consolation of Philosophy* is the work of a man whose world has been shattered. Disgraced, his family's future threatened, condemned to death, he writes a book which fulfils what Plato considered to be the philosopher's true task: to prepare himself for death (Phaedo 67d–e).'[2] The image of the solitary prisoner, unjustly treated by a despot, left to an unknown fate, becomes the most resonant of objective correlatives to some of the themes and motifs.

In fact it is unlikely that Boethius was confined to a windowless hell-hole. He may have been allowed a few creature comforts and access to some books. But even if his surroundings were relatively humane, the prospect of death must surely have exercised his mind. It would have seemed ominous that he had been denied the opportunity to defend himself in person against the charges brought against him. Also, Theodoric, who had generally been a tolerant and enlightened ruler, was reported to have

1. 'Literary Design in the *De Consolatione Philosophiae*', in Gibson (ed.), *Boethius: His Life, Thought and Influence,* p. 237
2. O'Daly, *The Poetry of Boethius,* p. 236

become increasingly irascible and paranoid in his old age. The king's deteriorating relationship with the Eastern Roman emperor, Justin I, would not have helped his humour. (In the event Boethius was executed. One source says he was degradingly tortured then clubbed to death, another that he was, more mercifully, dispatched with a sword.)

Boethius's own physical imprisonment, therefore, is the shadowy presence behind the poems' exploration of mental and emotional captivity: 'But now he lies there, light of reason dead. / His neck's encumbered by such heavy chains' ('In the Dark', 1 m.2); 'Come here you prisoners of treacherous lust / Who's made a squat inside your earthy minds' ('Towards the Light', 3 m.10). The point reiterated in the poems is that imprisonment has nothing to do with physical restriction and everything to do with mental slavery: to the extent that people allow greed and lust to dominate their minds they will be unable to raise them up towards the divine light.

Lust, greed, vanity, fame, wealth are some of the chains that must be broken or avoided. Sensual pleasure is another, sharing the others' insatiability:

> All pleasures have the same capacity
> To spur you on but leave you hankering.
>
> Like bees who've poured out honey, pleasures flee
> And leave their stings inside you festering.

> ('Pleasure's Stings', 3 m.7)

It is the peril of the soul, imprisoned in the flesh, that Boethius returns to more fully in the story of Ulysses and Circe. Blown onto Circe's enchanted island, the Greek sailors drink her magic potion, which changes their physical forms into those of wild animals – a wild boar, lion, tiger, wolf – while still preserving their human consciousness. The moral, as Philosophy proclaims, is that Circe's sorcery was useless in that it could change the men's bodies, but not their hearts. By implication, the prisoner Boethius can take comfort that although his physical circumstances have changed for the worse, his mind is still free to seek the light of truth.

In a related theme Boethius considers the nature of power through the recurrent figure of the tyrant – a type that apparently stands in diametrical contrast to the 'prisoner' and which Boethius had been able to study closely through his proximity to Theodoric. In 'Nero's Legacy' (2 m.6), the poet makes the point that unbridled power exacerbates rather than reins in innate malevolence and depravity; and in 'True Honour' (3 m.4), he relates how the honours granted by the despotic Nero brought nothing but disrepute to the recipients – perhaps Boethius was now beginning to reevaluate the high honours Theodoric had conferred on him before his fall from grace. More tellingly, in 'Mental Tyrants' (4 m.2), Boethius points out that tyrants, who think they can control others by dint of force, are actually victims, controlled by their own greed, anger, hopes and sorrows. In the same way that the prisoner is only a prisoner in so far as he is controlled by his passions, a tyrant can only wield personal power in so far as he is free of those qualities that have driven him to be a tyrant in the first place. It is a point also emphasized in 'The View from Heaven' (4 m.1), in which the mind ascends to heaven and looks down on 'callous tyrants' left behind on earth and views them as 'exiles', alienated from themselves by the instincts that brought them to power. If Theodoric was able to incarcerate Boethius, he was impotent to control his prisoner's mental freedom; nor perhaps did the king have the power over his own imprisoning fears and anxieties that he would have liked. Such is part of Philosophy's consolation to the prisoner.

Another prominent motif that reflects Boethius's actual predicament is that of the movement from darkness – of captivity and the benighted mind – towards the light, the revelation of truth. Behind these images lie ideas from Platonic and Neoplatonic philosophy, which shone brightly in Boethius's intellectual firmament. In the former tradition there is, for example, Plato's allegory of the prisoners in the cave who watch a shadowy reality flickering on their cave wall. They eventually leave the cave and see the light of day and then the dazzling sun – a progression symbolizing the ascent to ultimate truth. In Neoplatonism, centered around the teachings of Plotinus, there is the idea of the individual soul descending from the ineffable One, the Good, the ultimate of three cosmic realities or 'hypostases' (the other two are Mind, and Soul), to the confines of the body. The body, however, is less a home than a prison – the soul's true home is the celestial realm of light from which it came and to which it yearns to return, dimly recollecting it through the barriers of the flesh.

Images associated with darkness and light are scattered throughout the poems. The moment when Boethius regains his vision after Philosophy's first soothing words is described in terms of an elemental force: 'Then if the north wind rushes from its cave / In Thrace, beats back the dark, unlocks the day / The sun so suddenly, so brilliantly bright / Now blinds our squinting eyes with dazzling light.' (1 m.3) In 'Orpheus in the Underworld' Boethius uses Orpheus's ultimate failure to retrieve Eurydice from the darkness of Hades to emphasize the need of the soul to be single-minded, to keep the 'path towards the sun' in its undeviating focus and to resist all temptation to look down towards the things of the earth. This ascent to the light of truth is spelled out in 'The View from Heaven' (4 m.1): by breaking free of the snares of the world and assuming Philosophy's 'wings', the mind can fly up to heaven, travelling through the ether and the stars of the Zodiac 'To join the sun god's path or journey with / Cold Saturn or with coruscating Mars' until it arrives at the realm where it can say

… This is my country, I remember!
From here I came – now here I've come to stay.

The theme of the mind's or soul's return to its rightful home is found not only in Plato and the Neoplatonists but also in the early Church. St Paul said that for as long as we are alive on earth we are conscious of being absent from God, and that 'we groan, longing to be clothed with our heavenly dwelling' (2 Corinthians 5:1–7). The Letter to the Hebrews refers to people being 'strangers' and 'aliens', or 'pilgrims', on earth, longing for a 'heavenly' country

(11:13–16). Boethius treats the subject most fully in 'Reverting to Type' (3 m.2). He presents four images from the natural world in two contrasting pairs to illustrate the innate tendency in things to yearn for and seek their natural state, just as the soul desires its true home. The first examples feature lions and a songbird taken into captivity. No matter how well tamed a lion may be, a sudden whiff of blood can send it into a state of primal, murderous savagery. No matter how well treated a caged songbird may be, if she glimpses her old woods she will pine and sing 'soft dirges' for them. The second pair of images, much shorter in length and stripped of elaboration, reinforce this theme: a sapling pulled towards the ground will spring back towards the sky when released; the sun sets in the west, but reappears as usual in the east – 'Each thing seeks out its own peculiar source.'

Instead of warring with each other, the disparate images of lion, bird, sapling and sun form patterns within a larger imaginative mosaic, the whole greater than the sum of its parts. They tease the mind into finding a unifying theme before, in the concluding lines, Boethius spells out the moral. Another, more terse, poet might have left the images to fend for themselves, for good or for ill. But Boethius is interested first and foremost in meaning, and clarity is one of his strengths, with his more explicit poetic statements feeding off carefully selected images, and vice versa.

Another major theme that was clearly at the forefront of Boethius's mind as he contemplated his spectacular fall from court favour is the apparent discrepancy between God's ordered universe and the lack of justice in human affairs. Some of his most elegant and rolling lines are used to describe cosmic harmony and the sense of order in nature, in which cycles of growth and decay are caused or coincide with natural forces or signs:

> The gentle west wind conjures leaves
> The north wind blew away: springs seeds
> Become the corn that Sirius burns.

('Lord of the Universe', 1 m.5)

There is a time for everything: in 'The Divine Order' (1 m.6) violets must be picked in spring and not in autumn, which is the time for the grape harvest. In a world ruled by love, the sun lights up the day, the moon the night; the seas and land observe each other's dominions ('Love's Laws' 2 m.8). Given this easily observed harmonious reality, what rankles with Boethius – and Job would have sympathized – is why people of impeccable moral probity are persecuted, while evil men are rewarded and prosper. One of the responses Philosophy gives to this conundrum lies in the nature of Fortune herself, who dispenses good and bad luck at whim. The trick is to reject her value system altogether. Once you have accepted and revelled in good luck (and Boethius had not only enjoyed high office but had had the signal honour of witnessing his two sons being made joint consuls by Theodoric) then it is only right that you must be prepared to endure the inevitable change of circumstance as Fortune turns her wheel. See Fortune for what she is and you break free of her power:

Fortune revolves her wheel as wilfully
As water surging up and down a creek:
Swatting once-feared monarchs cruelly

Raising the vanquished ... only for a while.
She's deaf to cries, untouched by human grief;
The groaning she provokes just makes her smile.

It's her hobby – how she proves her power
Impressing people with the marvellous trick
Of conjuring gloom from joy within an hour.

('Fortune's Wheel', 2 m.1)

Another response (set out in Book IV) is that the wicked only *seem* to prosper and that in fact their evil acts only serve to degrade their humanity and turn them into animals: the wicked are to be pitied rather than resented. Also, people judge evil acts with a limited perception. Philosophy explains that the workings of Fate may appear to bring about negative events. But these, because they are ultimately part of God's providential scheme, can have positive results – adversity may strengthen a person's character. People do not have the capacity to see the intricate workings of God's plan. They must trust that all is for the good, and that what may seem like the misfortunes of Fate are really part of the ordered pattern of Providence.

This issue of looking at things from human and divine perspectives informs the last and best-known theme of the *Consolation* (in Book V): the apparent discrepancy between God's providential scheme for the universe and his fore-knowledge of events and the ability of humans to act freely of their own accord. In essence, the problem is this: if God knows that I am going to watch a chariot race tomorrow, surely this means that I must necessarily do so – for if I chose not to go it would imply that divine omniscience is fallible. Philosophy's solution hinges on the difference between human and divine modes of perception and the nature of time. God, by virtue of being eternal, sees all worldly events – past, present, and future – as if they were all taking place at the same time in the present. And the fact that he can see them does not mean to say that they are necessary – that there is somehow a causal connection – in the same way that someone watching the sun rise does not cause it to do so.

THROUGHOUT the poems, as with the book as a whole, Boethius works his way through some of life's greatest conundrums to understand his ominous predicament better, drawing on the wisdom of the greatest classical thinkers. It has often been asked why Boethius, a committed Catholic Christian who had written a number of theological tractates, focused on pagan philosophy and not his religious faith for consolation at a time when his life was in the balance. For although there is little in the book that a Christian could object to, there are no unambiguous references to Christianity either (there may be the occasional indirect reference, for example the poem about building a home on sound foundations echoes Jesus's saying about the wise man who built his house upon a rock in Matthew 7:24–25). Was it that, like his image of the lions who revert to type on contact with blood, Boethius reverted to deeply

23

embedded pagan instincts when it came to the crunch?

There are too many gaps in our knowledge to speculate confidently. C. S. Lewis thought that Boethius may not have believed he was in danger of being executed when he wrote his book and that the consolation he sought was for his ruin rather than his imminent death. However, it is hard to imagine that part of Boethius, at the very least, was not prepared for the worst. Perhaps in fact he was constantly praying to the Christian God for deliverance or succour but simply preferred not to write about it at this time? Or did his mind prefer to immerse itself in the intricacies of existential questions and Philosophy's traditional classical response to them, sensing that Christian doctrine could not have elicited the same level of concentrated mental engagement to fill those long, silent apprehensive days?

In any case, it is Philosophy's, not Theology's, consolation that Boethius receives: how effective is it? Quite apart from the book as a whole, the poems give satisfying consolation in two ways. On the one hand, they constantly, naggingly even, point out the insubstantiality of human values and the futility of human achievements – traditional themes given extra sharpness by the verse forms and the poignancy of the poet's actual situation; on the other hand, they positively affirm the transcendent realm to which the soul must return. Poem by poem the emphasis shifts to different aspects of these themes, sometimes scrutinizing details, sometimes presenting overviews, until by the end the reader has risen above earth-clinging mists and gained a genuine glimpse of the world *sub specie aeternitatis*, and with it a liberating detachment and serenity as the various travails of existence are put into true perspective. By the end, the prisoner Boethius seems to realize that his captivity is of the body only and that his soul, by shaking off self-pity, fear, anxiety and resentment, can rise up to the One, an aspiration that finds its most inspirational expression at the end of 'Hymn to the Creator' (3 m.9):

Father, lift up our minds to your great throne
That we may contemplate the source of goodness;
And grant us that we may discover light
To gaze on you with clarity of vision.
Disperse the heavy fogs of this dense earth
Reveal yourself in all your shining glory!
To us who praise you and who aim to see you
You are the source of peace and gentle rest;
You are the start, you carry us and lead us
You are the path to truth, you are the end.

JAMES HARPUR

In Prison

I used to relish scribbling poetry.
But now I'm stuck with dirges born of sadness.
Look how the Muses, dishevelled by distress,
Prompt elegies that only make me cry.

At least they weren't put off by any fears
From being my companions on this journey.
They were the best thing of my salad days:
Now they console me in my sad last years.

A sudden spate of suffering and I'm old.
Decrepit from the tyrannous rule of anguish;
My hair's a snowdrift, prematurely white,
And flesh flaps off my clapped-out bones in folds.

Death's welcome when it passes by your prime
Arriving when you're begging for release.
But Death has turned a deaf ear to my prayers,
Won't close my red-rimmed eyes a final time.

When flighty Fortune brought me passing pleasure
I nearly came to grief at one dark point;
Now that her misty scheming face has changed,
My blasted life drags on at painful leisure.

Why did my friends harp on about my luck?
I stood on shaky ground: I came unstuck.

[1 m.1]

In the Dark

*'Gazing at my grief-dejected furrowed face, Philosophy
deplored my chaotic mind.'* – DE CONS. 1.1.14

Just look at him! his mind has sunk deep down,
Has lost its inner light, become so dull;
It reaches out towards external darkness
Each time a toxic wave of worry swells
Into a tsunami, launched by worldly gales.

This was the man who loved the open heavens
And journeyed down the trackways of the skies.
He'd study rose-red suns and icy moons
And calculate the planets' sinuous paths,
Subjecting them to mathematic laws.

This was the man devoted to enquiring
Why roaring hurricanes assault the sea
What spirit turns the sphere of the fixed stars
And why the sun climbs from the smouldering east
Then drops beneath the waters of the west;

And what ensures the gentle days of spring
Become so temperate that rosebuds pop
And multiply their beauty through the land;
And who at harvest when the time is ripe
Endows the autumn with its swollen grapes.

Revealing nature's secrets was his life.
But now he lies there, light of reason dead.
His neck's encumbered by such heavy chains
His head is forced to loll towards the ground
To contemplate the uninspiring mud.

[I m.2]

Light Returns

'Using a fold of her dress, Philosophy wiped away
the tears brimming in my eyes.' – DE CONS. 1.2.6

Night scattered, the sense of darkness went,
My eyes regained their power, just as when

Northwesterlies build clouds up into mountains,
Skies blacken, the atmosphere grows dim,

The sun's wiped out, the stars have not appeared
And night pulls down its curtain everywhere;

Then if the north wind rushes from its cave
In Thrace, beats back the dark, unlocks the day

The sun so suddenly, so brilliantly bright
Now blinds our squinting eyes with dazzling light.

[1 m.3]

A Calm Mind

'I hope for nothing, I fear nothing. I am free.'
— Epitaph of Nikos Kazantzakis

If you can bring presumptuous fate to bay
    By keeping calm and cultivating order,
Look fluctuating Fortune in the eye
    Unflinchingly, maintaining your composure:
The rabid sea exploding waves from deep,
    The bursting forges of Vesuvius
And lightning that can crack a castle keep
    Will be unable to disturb your peace.

Are human beings so wretched that they'll cower
    Before mad autocrats who rant in vain?
To neutralize their anger of its power,
    Surrender hope and keep your fear in train.
For if you're rattled by desire and dread
    And waver, having no self-mastery,
You've thrown away your shield – deserted
    To link the chain that drags you into slavery.

[1 m.4]

Lord of the Universe

'The moon marks off the seasons
and the sun knows when to go down.'

– PSALM 104:19

Creator of the glittering skies,
From your eternal throne you spin
The heavens with a mighty twist
And make the stars obey your law.

So, mirroring the fiery sun
The full moon blots out lesser lights
But then her glowing crescent fades
As she moves closer to his flames.

You make the frosty evening star
Appear when light begins to dim
And then you change his tack so he
Becomes the pastel star of morning.

You ration daylight miserly
When leaves cascade in bitter winter;
But make the night race through its hours
During the heatwaves of the summer.

Your hand controls the changing seasons:
The gentle west wind conjures leaves
The north wind blows away; spring seeds
Become the corn that Sirius burns.

Nothing escapes your ancient law –
All carry out their proper tasks;
You govern and set down the limits
To everything but human acts.

How otherwise can slippery Fortune
Create a topsy-turvy world:
The innocent get sentences
That should be given to the guilty;

Everywhere criminals reside
In places of great influence;
Justice is just a parody
When evil tramples on what's good.

A shadow dims the light of virtue;
The good are slandered by the wicked,
Who camouflage deceit with lies
And perjure with impunity;

And when they get the urge to flex
Their muscles – it warms their hearts
To undermine and topple kings
Who terrorize their citizens.

O you who wove the bonds of life
Have mercy on this wretched world.
Do we play such a tiny part
In your great work that Fortune's waves

Can knock us one way then another?
O Lord restrain this rolling ocean,
Steady the earth with that same law
By which you rule unbounded heaven.

[I m.5]

The Divine Order

The constellation of the Crab
Inflicts oppressive summer heat
And those who then entrust their seeds
To soil the hostile furrows cheat
Of any crops, and they're compelled
To grub for acorns in the forest.

Who searches for spring violets
When woods glow red and north winds sing
Across the swaying grassy plains?
And if you crave ripe grapes, then spring
Is not the time to cut young vines:
Bacchus will bring you gifts in autumn.

To every season God assigns
The tasks that are appropriate.
He does not let his ordered rhythms
Become disrupted, inchoate:
Whatever leaves his changeless pattern
Catapults headlong into ruin.

[1 m.6]

To See the Truth

I

Behind black clouds
The stars cannot
Pour out their light.

South winds slam
And swirl the sea
So glassy waves
That were as still
As halcyon days
Are coarse and grainy
With rucked-up sand
And stop us seeing.

III

Meandering streams
That tumble down
The mountainside

Are often blocked
By fallen rocks.

IV

And so with you:
If you desire
To gaze upon
The truth, clear-eyed,
Walking straight
Along its path,
Discard your joy
Discard your fear
Abandon hope
Let sadness go.
If these things reign
The mind is haze
And trapped in chains.

[1 m.7]

Fortune's Wheel

'For certein, what that Fortune list to flee,
Ther may not man the cours of hire witholde.'

— CHAUCER

Fortune revolves her wheel as wilfully
As water surging up and down a creek:
Swatting once-dreaded monarchs cruelly

Raising the vanquished … only for a while.
She's deaf to cries, untouched by human grief;
The groaning she provokes just makes her smile.

It's her hobby – how she proves her power
Impressing people with the marvellous trick
Of conjuring gloom from joy within an hour.

[2 m.1]

The Need for More

'But lay up for yourselves treasures in heaven.'

— MATTHEW 6:20

I

If Plenty plunged
Her hand inside
Her brimming horn,
Kept doling out
As many riches
As grains of sand
The sea rolls up
Or points of light
In starry skies
Nevertheless
We would not cease
From hurling out
Reproachful cries.

II

God may shower gold
On those who pray for it,
Reward the bold

With fame and honour, yet
His gifts will seem like straw.
Remorseless greed devours
Everything it finds
Then pants for more.

III

How do you keep in check
Obsessive cravings
When even those who stuff
Themselves with riches
Cannot get enough?

IV

You'll never be a man of wealth
If you imagine you are poor
And fret away your health.

[2 m.2]

Flux

'*Everything flows.*' – HERACLITUS

'*How quickly the world's glory passes away!*'
– THOMAS À KEMPIS

The sun god in his rose-flecked chariot
    Colours the dawn with spreading light
And faces of the fading stars grow pale
    Before the onslaught of his flames.
The temperate west wind ushers in the spring
    And groves become a blur of pink;
But if the ravening south wind runs amok, then
    It destroys the glorious blackthorn.
The sea is often like a glowing sheet
    Until the north winds make it seethe.

Since nature's beauty rarely stays the same
    But goes through changes all the time
Have faith in short-lived wealth, and put your trust
    In riches that will turn to dust!
The only constant that God's law has fixed
    Is that no constancy exists.

[2 m.3]

Sound Foundations

If you are shrewd and want to live
In a strong enduring dwelling place
That shrugs off shrilling easterlies,
Safe from the snarl of ocean's waves

Don't build it on a mountain top
Exposed to driving southern winds
Nor on dry sands that shift and drop
Beneath the pressure of the weight.

Shun beautiful but risky sites
And build it lower down on stone;
Then even if a thunderous cyclone
Rips up the sea and makes it writhe

Rooted in your tranquillity
Secure behind your sturdy walls
You'll live in peace contentedly
And chuckle at the vicious squalls.

[2 m.4]

The Golden Age

Blessed was that age so long ago
When people willingly placed trust
In fields that never let them down.

No enervating luxury
Prevailed, and appetites were mild
And satisfied by piles of acorns;

Ideas of sweetening wine with honey
Were still unknown, as was the fashion
Of dyeing sheeny silks bright purple.

Soft grass ensured a restful sleep
Smooth-flowing streams were good to drink
And giant pine trees offered shade.

Ships' oars did not chop up the sea
Since traders did not seek new shores
With their exotic merchandise.

No bugle-blasts of war were heard;
Blood spilled through bitter enmities
Had yet to stain the stubbly fields –

Why bother to provoke a fight
When gruesome wounds brought no reward?
If only people nowadays

Would embrace the ways of yesteryear!
But now the coals of avarice
Glow more intense than Etna's fire.

So curse whoever first unearthed
Such lethal treasures: gold-veined rocks
And gems that longed to stay untouched.

[2 m.5]

Nero's Legacy

We know the havoc he wreaked: Rome blazing,
Senators cut down, his brother murdered
And he steeped in his mother's blood appraising
Her corpse, dry-eyed. Sizing up its beauty.

Yet here was someone who was emperor
From farthest east to where the sun sinks down
From northern regions frozen by the Bear
To deserts where the parching south wind burns.

Was regal power impotent to soften
The blow of his insane depravity?
A grim affair, which happens all too often,
When lethal poison joins an unjust sword.

[2 m.6]

Double Death

'Let fame, that all hunt after in their lives,
Live register'd upon our brazen tombs,
And then grace us in the disgrace of death.'

— LOVE'S LABOUR'S LOST

'Scepter and crown
Must tumble down,
And in the dust be equal made,
With the poor crookèd sithe and spade.'

— JAMES SHIRLEY

All you who chase fame single-mindedly
As if it were the highest accolade
Should contemplate the vast estates of heaven
Compared with this backyard we call the earth:
    If even in this piffling world your name
    Means nothing, you'll be haunted by the shame.

Why do the arrogant attempt to shake
Their necks free from the yoke of Death in vain?
Their aura may spread wide and make tongues wag,
Great ancestors may gild their family tree;
    But such renown Death scorns: he makes a shroud
    For king and peasant, the humble and the proud.

Where are the bones of trusty old Fabricius?
Who knows where Brutus and stern Cato lie?

Only some small repute survives, a husk
Recorded by an all-too-brief inscription.
   And even if a person's name lives on
    It tells us nothing: only that he's gone.

You too will sink into oblivion.
No glory can establish your renown;
Do not assume your life can be prolonged
Because of your celebrity: the day
   Will come when this is also snatched from you.
   So what's in store is not one death, but two.

[2 m.7]

Love's Laws

'The love that moves the sun and other stars.' — DANTE

What power makes the universe produce
Harmonious change with such consistency?
What makes antagonistic elements
Maintain an endless truce between themselves ?
The sun's gilt chariot leads in the morning
The moon rules nights the evening star delivers.
The ocean muzzles all its slavering waves
So that the land preserves its boundaries.

It's love that keeps this chain of being steady,
Presiding over ocean, earth and sky —
If love relaxed its grip then straightaway
Those bound by common amity would slay
Each other, and destroy the trust they shared,
Built up by mutual faith and harmony.

The sacred law of love unites two nations.
Love binds the young in holy matrimony.
And love lays down the law that brings about
The friendship found between companions.
Think what a paradise this world would be
If love that rules the heavens ruled the heart.

[2 m.8]

Progressing to the Truth

To sow a field untouched by human hand,
First clear the undergrowth, scythe the ferns
And brambles, then new corn will fill the land.

You'll find that if you first taste something bitter
Honey is that much sweeter on the tongue;

The stars shine out with greater depths of glitter
When south winds clear away the drumming rains;

And when the morning star drives off the darkness
Horses light up the dawn with crimson manes.

You, too, have gazed upon false good: it's time
To make a start and throw off its constraints;
Allow the truth to creep inside your mind.

[3 m.1]

Reverting to Type

I

In a melodic song, with tinkling strings,
I'll sing how nature's hand steers everything
And how her providential law maintains
This universe by tying all its parts
With bonds that cannot ever come undone.

II

Though lions from Africa wear pretty chains,
Feed from their trainer's hand and fear his whip,
Blood only has to touch their shaggy jaws
And their ferocious dormant instinct wakes:
They now remember who they were – with roars
They snap their chains and shake them off their
        necks;
Their trainer is the first to feel their rage,
His bloody flesh now shredded by their fangs.

III

A songbird of the woods is shut inside
A cage, enjoys her owners' playful care,
Her honey-sweetened drink and mounds of food.
But if when flapping round her cell she spies
A sudden vista of her shady woods
She scatters food, hops up and down on it
And pining deeply for those trees alone
She sings soft dirges for her long-lost home.

IV

Bend back a sapling with all your might
Until its tip is on the ground, let go
And watch it spring towards the sky in flight.

V

The sun sinks down beneath the western seas
But then by travelling on a secret path
It reappears as usual in the east.

VI

Each thing seeks out its own peculiar source
And its return is cause for celebration.
Nothing retains the order it was given
Unless its end is joined to its beginning,
Ensuring that its cycle stays on course.

[3 m.2]

True Wealth

Rich people may enjoy their streams of gold,
Which always fails to satisfy their greed,

Stoop down from heavy strings of Red Sea pearls
And have a hundred oxen plough their fields

Yet worries still devour them while they live
And fickle wealth goes nowhere in the grave.

[3 m.3]

True Honour

Strutting around in purple and white pearls
Nero attracted everybody's hate
For a lifestyle that was cruel and lush.
He had the gall to give grand senators
Official posts that tarred them with his brush.

So who can think that someone's fortunate
When honoured by a thorough reprobate?

[3 m.4]

True Power

To gain true power, tame your violence:
Don't let yourself be steered by vile lust.

So what if India treats you as her master
Or if some distant land does what you ask her?

Unless you quit your grumbling and despair
You'll find your power nothing but hot air.

[3 m.5]

Divine Origins

'They that deny a God destroy man's nobility; for
certainly man is of kin to the beasts by his body; and,
if he be not of kin to God by his spirit, he is a base
and ignoble creature.'

— FRANCIS BACON

The human race arises from one source.
There is one father governing everything.
He gave the sun its fire, the moon its horns;
He filled the night with stars, the world with people
And placed celestial souls in mortal forms
So everyone would have a noble seed.

Why boast about your race or family tree?
Just think about your sacred provenance,
About your lord creator — then you'd see
That no-one is degenerate unless
He clings to vice and shuns his pedigree.

[3 m.6]

Pleasures' Stings

All pleasures have the same capacity
To spur you on but leave you hankering.

Like bees who've poured out honey, pleasures flee
And leave their stings inside you festering.

[3 m.7]

Blind Search

*'Ye shall know the truth, and the truth
shall set you free.'* – JOHN 8:32

A pity that sheer ignorance
Seduces people down false trails.
No one would search for gold on trees
Or go to vines to pick off jewels

Or set up nets on mountain tops
To catch a fish to grace a meal,
Or trawl the ocean for a goat.
People know what the waves conceal

The best place for white sheeny pearls
Or molluscs full of purple dye –
The shores that have the choicest fish
And those where spiky urchins lie.

But when it comes to seeking out
The good, they're blind and ignorant
And grope for truth beyond the stars
While burying their heads in sand.

What prayer would suit these idiots?
Let them chase wealth, and honour too,

Then having struggled for the spurious
May they appreciate the true.

[3 m.8]

Hymn to the Creator

'Why does the world move in a circle?
Because it imitates the mind.' – PLOTINUS

'Open your eyes, and the whole world
is full of God.' – JACOB BOEHME

Lord, creator of the earth and heaven
You guide the world by everlasting reason
And commanded time to leave eternity.
You do not move, but set all things in motion;
Nor did any cause outside yourself
Compel you to create this world of flux –
But your innate form of the highest good
Unstinting in its generosity.

From a celestial plan you make creation.
Being supremely beautiful yourself
You hold a world of beauty in your mind
And base our world upon this heavenly vision,
Commanding it to be a perfect whole
Through the perfection of its different parts.

You bind the elements together with your laws,
So cold may join with hot, and dry with wet,
And fire is not so pure it flies away
Nor earth so dense it sinks beneath the sea.

You made the soul, which moves all things,
The bridge between the mind and matter,
And you spread the soul throughout the universe
Among its parts, which work in harmony.

The soul's divided in two circular forms,
Each one returning to itself; and it
Encircles mind within the depths of being
And turns the heavens in a similar circle.
Likewise you bring forth souls and lesser beings
And placing them within light chariots
You scatter them in heaven and on earth.
By your benevolent law you bring them back
And they, by means of fire, return to you.

Father, lift up our minds to your great throne
That we may contemplate the source of goodness;
And grant us that we may discover light
To gaze on you with clarity of vision.
Disperse the heavy fogs of this dense earth
Reveal yourself in all your shining glory!
To us who praise you and who aim to see you
You are the source of peace and gentle rest;
You are the start, you carry us and lead us
You are the path to truth, you are the end.

[3 m.9]

Towards the Light

Come here you prisoners of treacherous lust
    Who's made a squat inside your earthy minds
And shamelessly has kept you tied up fast.
Here there is relief from all your struggling
    A sanctuary of calm abiding peace,
The only refuge open to the suffering.

The golden riches in the Tagus' sands
    Or from the River Hermus' ruddy soil,
Or all the lustrous pearls and emeralds
Scattered along the hot banks of the Indus
    Cannot illuminate the inner vision
But fill the blinded mind with their own darkness.

Whatever stimulates, enchants the senses
    Is nurtured in the bowels of the earth.
But the glory that guides and drives the heavens
Avoids the shadowy wreckage of the soul:
    Whoever gazes on this radiance
Will find the dazzling rays of sunlight dull.

[3 m.10]

Recollecting Truth

'There is an inmost centre in us all,
Where truth abides in fullness; and around,
Wall upon wall, the gross flesh hems it in …'

— ROBERT BROWNING

Whoever hunts the truth wholeheartedly
Refusing to be tempted down false trails
Must turn his inner light upon himself,
Bring into focus all his rambling thoughts
And teach his mind the wealth it seeks outside
Lies waiting in its treasury within.
    Then what has just been hidden by the haze
    Of error shines brighter than the sun's own rays.

Though flesh weighs down the mind, makes it forget,
It cannot drive out every trace of light –
Because the spark of truth adheres inside
And flares to life when fanned by winds of learning.
Suppose you're asked a question: how can you
Reply correctly and spontaneously
Unless you had some inkling deep within?
    If what the Muse of Plato said was true
    We learn what we've forgotten we once knew.

[3 m.11]

Orpheus in the Underworld

Blessèd was he who could behold
The coruscating fount of goodness;
Blessèd was he who could undo
The chains that heavy earth imposes.

When Orpheus mourned Eurydice
His dirges made the forests move
And stopped the rivers in their tracks;
The deer lay down beside the lion
The hare no longer feared the hounds
Quiescent from the lulling music.
But when his grief intensified
Smouldering deep within his breast
When music that had conquered nature
Could not console the music maker
Orpheus harangued the savage gods
And went down to the underworld.

There he played and sang divinely
And drew his inspiration from
His mother Calliope's stream,
From uncontrollable distress
From love redoubling his pain.

And having moved that hellish realm
He gently begged its lords for mercy.

Enraptured by such haunting tunes
Three-headed Cerberus fell silent
The Furies, whom the guilty dread,
Were overcome with grief, and wept;
The wheel of Ixion stopped revolving;
Tantalus felt no more desire
To quench his chronic thirst for water;
Delighting in those songs the vulture
No longer tore out Tityus' liver.

At last the king of hell cried out
Despairingly, 'This man has won!
We grant that he may take his wife
Away – his music has released her.
But we insist on one condition:
That while he's leaving Tartarus
He does not glance back on his way.'
Who can impose a law on lovers!
Love is its own superior law.
So, sadly, near the beckoning light
Orpheus looked back and when he saw
Eurydice … he lost her
And losing her, he lost himself.

The moral of the tale is this:
Whoever wants to lead his mind
Along the path towards the sun
If he succumbs and turns his eyes
Towards the cavernous underworld –
By looking backwards at the dark
He loses everything he's won.

[3 m.12]

The View from Heaven

'The function of the wing is to take what is heavy
and raise it to the region above, where the gods dwell.'

– PLATO

'There is another life, emancipated, whose quality is
progression towards the higher realm …'

– PLOTINUS

I have quick wings to fly you to the heavens
And when your nimble mind has put them on
It will despise the earth as something grim
And soar beyond the stretching realm of air
To see the clouds as tiny specks below.
Ascending through the upper realm of fire
That's heated by the ether's rapid movements
It rises to the starry Zodiac
To join the sun god's path or journey with
Cold Saturn or with coruscating Mars;
And where night glitters like a silver painting
It follows round the orbits of the stars.
Contented with its efforts up till now
It leaves the farthest limits of the sky
And stands upon the ether's outer boundary
Revelling in the awe-inspiring light.
For this is where the king of kings holds sway
Who holds the universe's reins and drives

Its speeding chariot – though he remains
Unmoved, the radiant lord of everything.

And if the path returns you to this place
Which you forgot but now attempt to find,
You'll say, 'This is my country, I remember!
From here I came – now here I've come to stay.'
And should you want to gaze down on the world
Of darkness that you left, you'll see as exiles
Those callous tyrants who inspired such fear.

[4 m.1]

Mental Tyrants

*'What causes fights and quarrels among you? Don't
they come from your desires that battle within you?'*

−JAMES 4:1

Those mighty kings you see puffed up on thrones
In flashy purple, flanked by bristling weapons
And full of menace, wheezing frenziedly −
Just strip these proud men of their fripperies
And you'd see the chains constricting them inside.
Lust makes their pulses race with poisonous greed
Tumultuous waves of anger beat their minds, and
Slippery hope torments them, sorrow grinds them.

So when you see a head that's full of tyrants
You know it's crushed and can't do what it wants.

[4 m.2]

Circe's Sorcery

*'What goes into a man's mouth does not make
him "unclean", but what comes out of his mouth …'*

— MATTHEW 15:11

The ships of Ulysses' fleet
Were buffeted about the sea
And driven by the southeast wind
Onto the island home of Circe
The lovely daughter of the sun.
She served her guests a witch's brew
With magic herbs that changed their forms:
So one looked like a wild boar
Another sprouted fangs and claws
As he became a Libyan lion;
One with the appearance of a wolf
Tried weeping but could only howl;
Another, with a tiger's body,
Crept tamely round the palace halls.

Mercury pitied Ulysses,
Beset by various different threats,
And rescued him from Circe's spell;
But his men had quaffed the poisoned drink
And now as swine they stuffed themselves
With acorns, not their usual bread.

Their voices, bodies, bore no trace
Of what they were: their minds alone
Remained the same, just as before,
Bemoaning their new brutish forms.
How useless was her sorcery!
How impotent her magic herbs!
Although prevailing over flesh
They could not influence the heart.
A person's strength resides within,
Where it is hidden and secure.
The poisons that are really deadly
Are those that find their way inside
And brutalise your inner being
Leaving your body as it is
While they completely wreck your mind.

[4 m.3]

Tempting Fate

Why is it we enjoy inciting passions,
Relish provoking fate with our own hands?
Why seek out Death, which closes in unasked,
Letting its horses gallop on ahead?
    The threat of lions, bears, tigers, boars
    And snakes is bad enough: why fight with swords?

Do we choose Death by someone else's weapon
And wage unjust and bloody wars because
Another people's ways just seem too 'foreign'?
How can we justify such violence?
    So, if you want to give each man his due
    Have pity on the wicked, love the true.

[4 m.4]

Revealing Causes

*'Blessed is he who has come to know
the causes of things.'* – VIRGIL

If you had no idea that the stars
Known as Arcturus glide beside the pole
Or why Boötes slowly drives his Wagon
Dipping his flames beneath the sea so late
   Yet quickly rising from the waves again –
   You'd be astounded by the law of heaven.

The full moon's face becomes a mask of night
Whenever it's eclipsed by creeping shadow:
Her light now blotted out, she sees the stars
Her brilliance had just before concealed.
   Then people in the grip of superstition
   Beat gongs to bring her brightness back again.

Yet no one wonders when the northwest wind
Smashes the shore with roaring rolling waves
Or when the burning rays of sun reduce
A frozen-solid mound of snow to slush –
   For here on earth the causes are quite clear:
   The mysteries of the skies create the fear.

So anything at all unusual
Or occurring unexpectedly
Is bound to make the fickle masses gasp.
But if the cloudy layers of ignorance
   Evaporated, what inspired such awe
     Would not seem quite so marvellous any more.

[4 m.5]

The Love that Binds Creation

'The heavens declare the glory of God;
and the firmament sheweth his handywork.'

– PSALM 19:1

To see God's laws with clarity of mind
Look up and view the glittering roof of heaven
Where by his just and universal order
The stars preserve their immemorial peace.
The fiery mass of sun does not impede
The moon, who drives her chariot of ice;
The Bear moves swiftly round the pole of heaven
But never plunges to the western sea
Nor wants to touch the ocean with its flames
Despite observing other stars sink down.
With constant regularity of rhythm
The evening star leads in the gathering dusk
Then as the morning star brings back the day.

So in this way reciprocating love
Creates anew the world's eternal cycles
And strife is exiled from the starry shores.
This concord keeps the elements in balance:
Wet gives way to dry, its opposite,
And cold is reconciled with burning heat.
Flickering fire flares upwards in the air
While earth subsides by virtue of its weight.

And this is why when spring brings in its warmth
The year will blossom in a scent of flowers
Why summer heat will parch the fields of corn
Why autumn trees return with heavy fruits
And winter is awash with nagging rain.
This changing of the seasons nourishes,
Creates all living things that breathe on earth
But then it snatches back and buries them
And bears them off when they have passed away.

Meanwhile the Maker sits on his high throne
Ruling the universe and guiding it.
For he is king and lord, the fount and source,
He is the law, wise arbiter of justice.
Of all the things that he has set in motion
He halts and brings back those that go off course;
For if he did not set them back on track
Compelling them again to keep their cycles
Then everything now held in constant order
Would break apart, divided from its source –
Which is the love that all things share in common
The final good they hope will bind them.
The only way that they can hope to last
Is if, with love again attracting them,
They stream back to the one that gave them life.

[4 m.6]

The Way of the Hero

'It lies in your power to create the sort of fortune that you want.' – DE CONS. 4.7.22

I

Ten years of waging war and Agamemnon
Avenged his brother's desecrated marriage
By ruthlessly reducing Troy to dust.
When desperate for his boats to put to sea
He bought fair winds, but at a bloody cost:
Switching his role from father to grim priest
He had to cut his wretched daughter's throat.

II

Ulysses mourned his dead companions
When Polyphemus reclining in his cave
Brusquely stuffed them in his bloated gut.
But when the giant, blinded, raged and raved
He paid for his delight with stinging tears.

III

Twelve gruelling tasks gave Hercules his fame.
He brought to heel the overbearing centaurs;

Skinned the ferocious lion of Nemea;
Downed the Stymphalian birds with deadly arrows;
Stole apples from beneath the dragon's nose
And carried back the gold in his left hand;
He chained and dragged up Cerberus from hell;
He caught, it's said, the mares of Diomedes
And fed them with their cruel master's flesh;
He burned to death the Hydra and her poison,
And broke a horn off Acheloüs' head
Making him hide in shame below his banks;
He toppled huge Antaeus on Libyan sands;
Killed Cacus for the sake of King Evander;
His shoulders – soon to bear the universe –
Were soaked in spittle when he slew the boar;
And, last, he lifted up the firmament
With his unflinching neck and for this task
He was rewarded with a place in heaven.

IV

So come, brave travellers, strike out along
The high road taken by these great exemplars –
Don't let inertia make you turn your backs!
If you can conquer earth you'll win the stars.

[4 m.7]

Law of Chance

'If everything is ordered by God,
no random events are possible.' – DE CONS. 5.1.8

The Tigris and Euphrates have one source
That bubbles from the rocky heights of Persia,
Where fleeing Parthians turn to shoot pursuers,
But soon their waters take a separate course.

Yet if they joined again and formed one stream
Then everything transported by each river –
Ships and uprooted trees – would come together
And the mingled waters flow haphazardly.

And yet topography and downward flow
Would still control the random swirling currents.
So chance, which seems to run with loosened reins,
Bites on the bit, and must obey the law.

[5 m.1]

The True Sun

Homer sang sweetly how the brilliant sun
Can 'see and hear all things' with its pure rays;
Yet it is still too weak to penetrate
The bowels of the earth or depths of seas.

The architect of this great universe
However, sees everything from a great height:
He's unconstrained by any mass of earth
Or clouds materializing in the night.

With one swift glance his mind can apprehend
What was, what is, and what's about to come.
Since he can see all things, and he alone,
It's fair to say that he's the one true sun.

[5 m.2]

The Whole and Parts

'*Without the Truth there is no knowing.*'
— THOMAS À KEMPIS

What spirit of discordance breaks apart
The bonds that hold the universe in place?
What god has thrust two truths against each other
So though each one can stand up by itself
When they are joined they cannot stay together?
Or is there never war between two truths
And they are always firmly interlocked?

Or is it that the mind engrossed by flesh
Cannot discern with its faint flickering light
The subtle links connecting everything?
Yet why then does it have a burning need
To recognise the inner signs of truth?
Does it know what it frets to know so much
(But who would toil to know what's known!);
Yet if it does not know, why seek things blindly?
For who would seek something in ignorance?
Who would pursue a thing that was unknown?
How would you find it? How would you recognise
An object that you'd never seen before?

So when the mind gazed on the mind of God
Did it discern the whole and all its parts?
Though now it's muffled by its layers of flesh
The mind cannot forget itself completely
And still recalls the whole, if not the parts.
When seeking truth, you fall between two stools:
You do not comprehend the total picture
Nor are you altogether in the dark.
Reflect upon the whole that you remember
And contemplate the things you saw in heaven
Then you can add to what you have retained
The other parts that you have now forgotten.

[5 m.3]

The Vital Mind

There used to be some fusty Stoic thinkers
Who thought that sense impressions from outside
Are imprinted on our minds as images,
Just as it was the custom in the past
To press out letters deftly with a stylus
Onto a pristine page of virgin wax.

But if the mind's own vital energy
Creates nothing, but simply lies there slack,
Receiving stimuli from things, reflecting
Appearances alone, just like a mirror,
Where does it get its overriding sense
Of being able to discern all things?

What mental power sees things separately
Or breaks down knowledge into various strands?
What mental force reintegrates these strands
And alternates between two different paths –
Now raising thoughts up to the highest sphere
And now descending to the world below –
Then turning inwardly for self-reflection
To contradict the false with what is true?

This power is far more forceful and effective
Than that which simply waits for sense impressions.
And yet some prompting of the body precedes
And stimulates the powers of the mind
As when light hits the eyes, or noise the ears:
Then mind stirs into action, conjures up
The most appropriate of its inner forms
And matches up the images received
With its repository of forms inside.

[5 m.4]

Higher Vision

How varied are the creatures of this earth!
Some sweep the dust with elongated bodies,
Their muscular bellies pressing out a trail.
Some beat the air, and drifting on light wings
Glide smoothly through the open tracks of space.
Some like to leave their footprints in the soil
When skirting woods and crossing grassy plains.

Although these creatures differ in appearance
They look towards the ground, which dulls their senses.
For only humans hold their heads erect
And from this upright stance can scorn the earth.
Unless you are a crass materialist
Your form should tell you as you strain to gaze
At heaven, forehead lifted to the sky,
To raise your mind up too, in case weighed down
It sinks below your body raised up high.

[5 m.5]

Boethius's Life

BORN IN ROME in about AD 480, Boethius was a member
of the Anicii clan, an aristocratic family that had been
Christian for more than a century. Orphaned when still a
young boy, Boethius was adopted by a noble named
Quintus Aurelius Memmius Symmachus, one of Rome's
wealthiest and most cultured men, who ensured he
received an excellent education. In fact Boethius became
so fluent in Greek – a relatively rare achievement among
Romans at this time – and learned in Platonic philosophy
that scholars have speculated whether he spent some time
at Athens or Alexandria (for which there is no direct
evidence). In time he married Symmachus's daughter
Rusticiana, who bore him two sons.

A man of great intellect and integrity, Boethius
inevitably attracted the attention of Theodoric, the
Ostrogothic king of Italy who nominally recognized the
eastern Roman emperor, based at Constantinople, as his
overlord (the last western Roman emperor had been
deposed in 476). The diversity of Boethius's talents is
shown by the fact that Theodoric commissioned him to
investigate the debasement of coinage and to make a
water-clock and sundial to send to the king of the
Burgundians. In 510 Boethius received the honour of
being appointed sole consul, following in the footsteps of
his father and Symmachus. But his real passion was for the

affairs of the mind, not the state. He studied mathematics, geometry, astronomy and music, subjects that formed the *quadrivium* (a word he coined) of the medieval education system, and some of his treatises on them became set texts. He ambitiously embarked on translating the complete works of Plato and Aristotle, along with commentaries, hoping eventually to reconcile their ideas – a project he had made only small inroads into by the time of his death. But it was thanks to his translations of Aristotle's works on logic that these were known in the later Middle Ages. He also wrote five tractates on Christian theology, which demonstrate his impeccably orthodox faith (a fact that may have perturbed Theodoric, who was a Christian of the heretical Arian variety).

In about 522 Boethius reached the pinnacle of his career when his two sons were appointed joint consuls – an extraordinary honour both for them and their father – and he himself was appointed Master of Offices, a highly influential administrative position at Theodoric's court. Yet, within a year or so, Boethius's world sensationally collapsed when he was accused of treason and of practising 'magical arts'. The principal charge, that of treason, came about when a senior Roman senator named Albinus was accused of writing to the eastern emperor, Justin I, in a way that was disloyal to Theodoric. Relations between the Arian Theodoric and the orthodox Justin had been deteriorating, so the allegations were serious. When Boethius stepped in to defend Albinus he found himself tarred with the same brush: he was arrested and imprisoned in Ticinum (Pavia), near Milan, in about 524. During his confinement he wrote the *Consolation*. At some point before Theodoric's own death in August 526 Boethius was executed. His father-in-law Symmachus suffered the same fate. Buried in Pavia, Boethius became worshipped locally as St Severinus from at least the ninth century. In 1883 the Church formally approved his cult.

APPENDIX II

A Summary of the Five Books
of the *Consolation*

BOOK I

THE SCENE OPENS with Boethius, the prisoner, bemoaning his fate. Philosophy, in the guise of a woman, appears to him and dismisses the attendant poetic Muses who, she claims, have exacerbated Boethius's distress. She encourages him to air the cause of his misery, and he duly pours out his heart, recounting his good deeds as a statesman and the injustice of the accusations made against him. He feels that there is injustice in the world, with the good receiving the punishments that the wicked deserve. Philosophy responds that he is not only exiled from his home, but from his true self. Proposing to administer gentle medicine to prepare him for more powerful remedies, she begins to probe his state of mind. She ascertains that although Boethius is still able to affirm that God is the source of life and watches over his creation, he, Boethius, does not know his own true nature nor the purpose of things and events and so believes the world is governed by capricious Fortune.

BOOK II

PHILOSOPHY outlines to Boethius the nature of Fortune, pointing out that the latter's fickleness is not something to resent: it is an essential part of her character. To commit oneself to the jurisdiction of Fortune means having to accept the misfortunes that come about as she turns her wheel. Philosophy chides Boethius for his self-pity and reminds him of all the success and happiness that he has enjoyed until his fall. He must accept that there is no constancy in life and that people never enjoy perfection – for example people blessed with wealth may be lonely or childless: happiness cannot be found in external things governed by chance; it can be found only within. The idea that people can, as it were, appropriate beautiful or precious things to glorify themselves is false – fine clothes will reflect favourably on the tailor, not the wearer. Similarly, power and fame are relative, transient qualities.

BOOK III

BY NOW Boethius's spirits are beginning to revive and he is eager to hear more of what Philosophy has to say. Philosophy explains that people vainly search for happiness, the perfect good, through wealth, artistic endeavour, pleasure, fame and power, which are false goods because they cannot guarantee happiness. She then attempts to show what true happiness is: that it is by nature an undivided whole, simple, self-sufficient – the perfect good which is to be identified with God, than whom nothing better can be conceived. People can become happy by participating in the essence of happiness, the good, that is God, and all things have a natural inclination towards Him. God is omnipotent and rules the universe and can do no evil, which is 'nothing', since what God cannot do cannot be said to be anything.

BOOK IV

BOETHIUS now asks Philosophy why evil can flourish in a world controlled by a good God. She replies that all people seek happiness: the good seek it through virtue, the bad through their desires. The bad fail to find it because by departing from their true nature they forego their humanity and become subhuman, i.e. animals. Paradoxically, the wicked are happier when they receive punishment because it is a just measure and therefore good for them. The wicked should be seen as sick, in need of medicine and sympathy rather than blame.

The focus then switches to the relationship between Providence and Fate. the two are inextricably tied together or rather represent two aspects of the same phenomenon. Providence, divine reason, controls the destinies of people through the workings of Fate: God has arranged it that the immutable plan of Providence is worked out in detail by Fate. To avoid getting caught up in the 'chains of Fate' it is necessary to move closer to the primary stability and simplicity of Providence. People cannot always discern the workings of Fate, which is subject to Providence, and so do not realize that evil acts may eventually lead to good outcomes: people must trust that God has ordered the world providentially even if they do not comprehend how.

BOOK V

IN THE LAST book, Philosophy explains the apparent conflict between providence and divine foreknowledge and people's free will. Does the fact that God knows something is going to happen mean that it must necessarily happen and people are helpless to change it? To begin with Philosophy, drawing on Aristotle, considers the nature of chance and how it occurs when unforeseen causes collide, as when a man buries gold in a field and, later, another man digging for some purpose happens to find the gold. She then affirms the reality of free will, which is dependent on a person's ability to shun vice (for vice destroys the reason to exercise free will). Philosophy tackles the foreknow-ledge versus free will issue by outlining the modes by which things are comprehended – i.e. by sense, imagina-tion, reason and, lastly, divine intelligence. Through the latter God, who resides in eternity, can see the temporal events of the world as if they were all happening in the present: for him, unlike for humans, there is no distinction between past, present and future. And just because he sees what, for us, are future events does not mean that they will necessarily happen, any more than our watching the sun rise compels the sun to do so.

Select Bibliography

Barrett, H. M. *Boethius: Some Aspects of His Times and Work* Cambridge, 1940

Chadwick, H. *Boethius: The Consolations of Music, Logic, Theology, and Philosophy* Oxford, 1981

Cooper, W. V. *Boethius: The Consolation of Philosophy* London, 1902

Gibson, M. T. (ed.) *Boethius: His Life, Thought and Influence* Oxford, 1981

James, H. R. *The Consolation of Philosophy of Boethius* London, 1897

Lerer, Seth *Boethius and Dialogue: Literary Method in the Consolation of Philosophy* Princeton, 1985

Lewis, C. S. *The Discarded Image* Cambridge, 1964

O'Daly, Gerard *The Poetry of Boethius* Chapel Hill and London, 1991

O'Donnell, J. J. *Boethius, Consolatio Philosophiae* Bryn Mawr 1984

Patch, H. R. *The Tradition of Boethius* New York, 1935

Relihan, Joel C. *Boethius: Consolation of Philosophy*, Indianapolis/Cambridge, 2001

Tester, S. J. *The Consolation of Philosophy* Cambridge, Mass., 1973

Walsh, P. G. *Boethius: The Consolation of Philosophy* Oxford, 1999

Watts, V. E. *Boethius: The Consolation of Philosophy* Harmondsworth, 1969

Index

Book 4

Book 5